TREMENDOUS TEXAS

TREMENDOUS TEXAS

Barbara Bartels

PREMIUM PRESS AMERICA
NASHVILLE, TENNESSEE

TREMENDOUS TEXAS by Barbara Bartels

Published by PREMIUM PRESS AMERICA

Copyright © 2002 PREMIUM PRESS AMERICA

ISBN 1-887654-52-6

Library of Congress Catalog Card Number 00-136411

PREMIUM PRESS AMERICA gift books are available at special discounts for premiums, sales promotions, fund-raising, or educational use. For details contact the Publisher at P.O. Box 159015, Nashville, TN 37215, or phone toll free (800) 891-7323 or (615)256-8484, or fax us at (615)256-8624.

For more information visit our web site at *www.premiumpressamerica.com*.

Typesetting by Bob Bubnis/BookSetters
Printed by Falcon Press

First Edition October 2002
1 2 3 4 5 6 7 8 9 10

Dedication

To Ron and George for their help, encouragement and patience.

Introduction

Big. Proud. Independent. Flat. Hot.

Sure, Texas is all of that—but more, **much** more. It's a state of many contrasts—from the high country of Big Bend to the sandy beaches of South Padre Island; from the silence at the Alamo to the raucous fans at a Texas Rangers' baseball game; from Spanish missions to Victorian houses to I. M. Pei buildings; from fields of bluebonnets to flesh-eating plants; from barbeque and chili cook-offs to *haute cuisine*; from art museums filled with paintings by Monet, Mondrian and Magritte to cave paintings by Native Americans. Texas has got something for everyone! Here's a bit of what makes Texas the unique place it is.

Y'all enjoy...

☆ TREMENDOUS TEXAS ☆

1. The name "Texas" derives from the Caddo Indian word *"tejas,"* which means "friends." The official state motto is "Friendship."

2. Texas is as large as all of New England, New York, Pennsylvania, Ohio and Illinois combined. Its area is 266,874 square miles, including 4,959 square miles of inland water. Its greatest east-west distance is 774 miles, while the greatest north-south distance is 737 miles. It ranks first in size among all the continental states.

3. Texas is called the "Lone Star State" because it has a single star on its flag.

4. Botanists have identified over 5,000 species of flowers indigenous to Texas. In early spring, many cities sponsor flower "tours" that offer visitors a chance to enjoy the state's many varieties of blooming plants.

5. Throughout its history, six different flags have flown over Texas, but governments have actually changed eight times: Spain (1519-1685); France (1685-1690); Spain (1690-1821); Mexico (1821-1836); Republic of Texas (1836-1845); United States (1845-1861); Confederate States of America (1861-1865); and United States (1865-present). Texas joined the Union for the first time on December 29, 1845. It's the only state to enter the United States by treaty instead of territorial annexation.

6. There are 33 different species of bats living in Texas (more than any other state), making bats the "Official Flying Mammal of Texas." Sounds awful, but the 1-1/2 million bats that live under the Congress Avenue Bridge in Austin are estimated to eat between 10,000 and 30,000 pounds of insects EVERY NIGHT! Now, that is quite a bug zapper!!

7. The capitol of Texas is Austin. Its capitol building opened on May 16, 1888 and has the distinction of being the largest capitol building in the nation. The main building covers 2.25 acres of ground with over eight acres of floor space. A four-story, 650,000 square foot underground extension was added in 1993. Constructed of pink granite, its dome rises seven feet higher than the dome of the nation's Capitol.

8. The Dallas Zoo has a nationally renowned African zoo exhibit. In a 25-acre tract featuring the six major African habitats, birds and mammals dwell in surroundings that resemble their native habitats. Their reptile house boasts one of the largest collections of rattlesnakes in the world!

9. The official state bird is the mockingbird that gets its name from copying the calls of many other birds and an occasional Texan.

10. Admiral Chester W. Nimitz, Commander in Chief of the Pacific Fleet during World War II, was born in Fredricksburg in 1885. His military career and stories of the war in the Pacific are chronicled at the Admiral Nimitz Museum in downtown Fredricksburg. An interesting feature of the museum is the Japanese Garden of Peace given to the museum by the nation of Japan.

11. Charles Goodnight, the most famous of the Texas cattlemen, was a popular guy. Why? Charles invented the chuck wagon! He and fellow cowboy Oliver Loving established one of the Southwest's most heavily used cattle trails, the Goodnight-Loving Trail.

12. Always wanted to see a two-headed cow and nine-legged goat? Then don't miss the oddities at the Buckhorn Saloon and Museum in San Antonio. Nobody does kitsch better than they do!

13. The missions of El Paso are the oldest in the country. The Yselta Mission, located in an El Paso suburb of the same name, dates back to 1681. In 1682 the Piro Indians helped to build the Socorro Mission, considered to be the longest running mission in the United States. A third mission, the San Elizario, was erected 100 years later as a presidio (fortified settlement) to provide protection from the hostile Indians in the area.

14. Windmills are dear to the hearts of Texans living on the windy plains. In the town of Littlefield, northwest of Lubbock on Highway 84, stands a 114-foot replica of what was once known as the world's tallest windmill. The original was built in 1887 and stood 132 feet high.

15. The largest body of water completely within Texas' boundaries is Sam Rayburn Reservoir in east Texas. It covers 113,400 acres.

☆ TREMENDOUS TEXAS ☆

16. According to the 1850 census, Texas had a population of 213,000. By 1900 that figure had grown to an amazing 3,000,000! And in 2000, the census reported 20,851,820 residents—an increase of 23% over the 1990 figure. Texas has 24 cities with more than 100,000 people. Houston is the largest (1,953,631), followed by Dallas (1,188,580), San Antonio (1,144,646), Austin (656,562), El Paso (563,662) and Fort Worth (534,694).

17. Three Indian reservations are in the state: the Alabama-Coushatta Reservation, located between Livingston and Woodville in east Texas; Yselta del Sur Pueblo (Tigua Indian Reservation), near El Paso; and the Kickapoo Reservation in Maverick County. Approximately 65,000 Native Americans live in Texas, ranking it sixth among all the states. However, most Native Americans in Texas do not live on reservations.

18. A few miles southeast of Luling, in Gonzales County, lies the unusual and interesting Palmetto State Park. It is named after the tropical palmetto (the state tree of South Carolina) that grows wild in the area along with other tropical plants. The 263-acre park resembles a tropical botanical garden.

19. Texas is home to many great athletes. Rafer Johnson was born in Hillsboro in 1935. He won the silver medal in the decathlon in 1956 and a gold medal in 1960. One of the greatest sprinters of all time was Bobby Jo Morrow from San Benito and Abilene Christian College. Morrow won three gold medals at the 1965 Melbourne, Australia Olympics. Chicago Cubs baseball team shortstop and Hall of Famer, Ernie Banks, is from Dallas. Another Hall of Famer, Nolan Ryan, known for his all-time record 5,714 strikeouts, was born in Refugio.

20. More than 100 of Texas' most well-known, deceased citizens were exhumed and moved to the little-used Texas State Cemetery in Austin for the celebration of its Centennial in 1936. First opened in 1851, it is now described as "a time capsule of Texas history." You can find the graves of Stephen F. Austin, Alamo survivor Susanna Dickinson and state flag designer Johanna Troutman there, among other distinguished Texas leaders.

21. About twenty miles northeast of Brenham is the Washington on the Brazos State Historical Park. The earliest moments of the Texas Republic are preserved there at a reconstructed version of Independence Hall. The Star Republic Museum is devoted to Texas history, as well. The restored home of the Republic's last President, Anson Jones, is on display. Great for all you history buffs!

22. The largest bronze monument in the world is at Pioneer Plaza in Dallas. There sit a collection of bronze, larger-than-life, longhorn cattle driven by three cowboys on horseback, as if in a cattle drive deep freeze.

23. Due to a freak of nature as well as a unilateral American decision, Texas increased in area and age at the end of the Mexican War. The oldest missions in the country, Yselta and Socorro, built on an island in the Rio Grand River in the 1680s, were abandoned in 1829 when the river flooded and shifted south. When the war ended in 1848, the peace treaty settled the boundary between Mexico and Texas at the center of the deepest channel of the Rio Grande. It was then that the U.S. discovered that the island and its missions were actually now north of the deepest channel, making them a part of Texas. Mexico was in no position to disagree, having just lost the war!

24. German-born, 19th-century sculptor Elizabeth Ney came to Texas from Europe in 1873 and eventually settled in Austin. She sculpted more than 100 busts of famous people in the United States, Texas and Europe. She is best known for her statues of Sam Houston, Stephen F. Austin, General Albert Sidney Johnson and Miriam A. Ferguson, Texas' first female governor, which can be seen at the Elizabeth Ney Museum in Austin.

25. The official small mammal of Texas is the armadillo. This amazing little animal is a relative of the sloth and anteater. All armadillos have shells, made of true bone, that cover their backs. But because their backs are covered with bone, armadillos are not very flexible. They rely on speed or their digging ability to escape danger. Watch those Texas highways for moving speed bumps!!

☆ TREMENDOUS TEXAS ☆

26. On November 22, 1963, President John F. Kennedy was assassinated while on a motorcade through Dallas. Texas Governor John Connolly, a passenger in the same car, was also wounded in his back and wrist. Vice President Lyndon B. Johnson, born near Johnson City, was sworn in as 36th president that same day.

28. On September 8-9, 1900, an estimated 6,000 of Galveston Island's 37,000 people were killed in a disastrous hurricane and flood. Winds of 120 mph drove a storm surge that submerged most of the island under 20 feet of water. It is regarded as the worst natural disaster ever in the United States.

29. At the Monastery of St. Claire near Brenham, the nuns support themselves by breeding miniature horses.

29. Gainesville, located in north Texas, has a zoo named after one of its own. Frank Buck ("Bring 'Em Back Alive Buck"), known as the Father of the Modern Era Zoo, has been honored since 1950 when the zoo opened, free of charge. Wonder if they have any of those miniature horses there?

30. The Texas Rural Heritage Center and Museum in Pittsburg contains a full-size replica of an airship designed around the turn of the century by Reverend Burrell Cannon. The original idea for the airship was based on a passage from the Book of Ezekiel that described a vehicle that was a "wheel within a wheel." Unfortunately, the original flying machine was destroyed in a railway accident as it was being transported to the 1904 St. Louis World Fair. The Optimist Club constructed the 26-by-23-foot replica.

☆ TREMENDOUS TEXAS ☆

31. When Texas was annexed in 1845, a resolution gave it the right to fly its flag at the same height as the national flag. That same resolution also gave Texas the right to divide into four states in addition to the original Texas. That legal right remains to this day.

32. Located between Austin and Houston, the small city of Round Top draws people from all over the world to it annual "Festival Institute," where classical musical students study with masters and put on concerts. During this summer festival, the community offers a series of instructional classes and professional and student concerts, making this destination internationally famous.

33. The first suspension bridge built in the U.S. was the Waco Bridge. Completed in 1870, the 475-foot pedestrian-only bridge still serves as a pedestrian crossing over the Brazos River.

☆ TREMENDOUS TEXAS ☆

34. Wichita Falls suffered irreparable damage when a tornado touched down on April 10, 1979. Three thousand homes were destroyed; 1,740 people were injured and 42 lives were lost, making this one of the worst natural disasters in Texas history.

35. Waco is the "Home of Dr Pepper." In 1885, at the Old Corner Drug Store, pharmacist Charles Alderton concocted the formula for this unique and famous soft drink. The manufacturing plant that first produced Dr (no period) Pepper still stands in downtown Waco.

36. Texas has more counties (254) than any other state. Forty-one counties in Texas are each *larger* than the state of Rhode Island. Rockwall County is the smallest county at 147 square miles. Brewster County is the largest at 6,204 square miles. Angelina County is the only one named for a woman.

37. Arlington, located between Dallas and Fort Worth, sounds like a great place for a family vacation. It is home to the Texas Ranger Baseball Club, Six Flags Amusement Park, Wild Water Center, Hurricane Harbor, Funsphere and the Mountasia Fantasy Golf Experience. A thrill a minute!

38. Texas is a spelunker's delight! Among the caves open to the public are the Cascade Caverns, north of San Antonio; the Inner Space and the Longhorn Cavern in central Texas and the Caverns of Sonora in southwest Texas. Be sure to bring lots of batteries!

39. During a 24-hour period in 1979, tropical storm Claudette dropped 43 inches of rain on the town of Alvin, located 20 miles south of Houston. This set a U.S. 24-hour rainfall record, but no one was applauding!

☆ TREMENDOUS TEXAS ☆

40. If you happen to be in Liberty at just the right time, you will hear a bell ringing from the Liberty Bell Tower. Liberty's bell is a replica of Philadelphia, Pennsylvania's famous bell. In fact, it was cast at the Whitchapel Bell Foundry in London, England, which was the same place that cast the cherished cracked-up one!

41. Fort Worth contains one of the finest museums in America. The Amon Carter Museum has over 358,000 items of American art, including paintings and sculptures created by Western artists Frederic Remington and Charles M. Russell and paintings by Winslow Homer, Grant Wood and Georgia O'Keefe. The museum also has a photography collection of 250,000 prints.

42. For a "peachy" good time drop by Weatherford during its Parker County Peach Festival. Held the second Saturday in July, it draws 25,000 peach lovers annually.

43. At Cadillac Ranch, outside Amarillo, ten battered Cadillacs are upended and buried in the dirt, their tail fins representing models from 1949 to 1963. Helium millionaire, Stanley Marsh III, who has encouraged graffiti artists, photographers and visitors to add their own "touches" over the years, owns this quirky exhibit.

44. Brady calls itself the "Heart of Texas" because it's the city closest to the actual geographic center of the state.

45. The King Ranch, located in south Texas, is bigger than the state of Rhode Island and largest of its kind in the world. It covers 825,000 acres and stretches over four counties: Nueces, Kenedy, Kleberg and Willacy. Established in 1853 by former riverboat captain Richard King, it still operates as a working ranch.

☆ TREMENDOUS TEXAS ☆

46. Pecos is the cantaloupe capital of Texas and celebrates with a festival each August.

47. On May 5, 1995, the most expensive thunderstorm in history hit the Dallas/Fort Worth area. Winds of 70 miles an hour, along with 3-5 inches of rain and large hail, pelted the area in sixty minutes. 109 people were injured and $2 billion of property was damaged by that one storm.

48. The oldest original existing courthouse in Texas sits in the town of Comanche in Comanche County. The log structure, affectionately known as "Old Cora,"(named after the original county seat) was built in 1856.

49. The town of Orange in east Texas is named after the groves of wild oranges that grow along the banks of the Sabine River. The Sabine marks the boundary between Texas and Louisiana.

50. The East Texas Oil Museum in Kilgore offers visitors a dramatic way to experience the oil boom of the 1920s-1930s. A simulated 3,800-foot elevator ride down into an oil formation gives folks an unusual perspective of oil production.

51. About 100 miles west of Houston lay the small communities of Dubina, Ammansville, High Hill and Praha. They share the distinction of having some of the most gorgeous "painted churches" in the nation. Besides high steeples and Art Nouveau interiors, they also contain stained glass windows, painted ceilings and other works of art.

52. A coastal live oak located in Lamar is called the Big Tree. It is believed to be more than 1,000 years old, is 35 feet in circumference, 44 feet tall and has an 89-foot spread. It is said to have been a council tree for the Carancahua Indians and is located in Goose Island State Park.

53. Sam Houston, one of Texas' most famous citizens, was actually born in Virginia. He served as governor of Tennessee before becoming President of the Republic of Texas.

54. In 1836, five sites served as temporary capitals of Texas: Washington on the Brazos; Harrisburg; Galveston; Velasco and Columbia. Sam Houston moved the capital to Houston in 1837. In 1839 the capital was moved to its present location, Austin.

55. James S. Hogg, the first native-born governor of Texas, easily won the Democratic nomination for governor in 1890 and went on to serve from 1891-1895. The six-foot two, two hundred eighty-five pound Hogg was a popular governor. His only daughter, Sarah Ann, affectionately known as "Miss Ima," (Ima Hogg!) became well known as a philanthropist.

56. The official state flower of Texas is the bluebonnet. Named for its color and resemblance of a woman's sunbonnet, the flower blooms in early spring, making Texas hillsides appear as endless seas of blue.

57. Houston's Astrodome was the first domed, climate-controlled stadium in the world when it was opened in April of 1965 and lends its name to astroturf which was first laid down there in 1966.

58. In 1848 soldiers were sent to Fort Martin Scott, the first federal fort built after Texas joined the Union. Charged with providing protection for the settlers in and around Fredricksburg, they discovered that the German settlers there had already made a treaty with the Comanches—one that was never broken by either side! Instead, the fort became a meeting place for all the area's residents to meet in peace.

59. Carthage is home to two of country music's greatest entertainers, Tex Ritter and Jim Reeves. Both men were born in this small community (pop. 6,500). A life-size statue of Reeves stands on U.S. Route 79, about three miles east of town. The Tex Ritter Museum in town displays all sorts of Ritter memorabilia.

60. Port Arthur is home to one of the most outstanding athletes of all time. Mildred "Babe" Didrikson Zaharias was an exceptional track star, earning two gold medals and one silver medal in the 1932 Olympics. She was also a golf legend, securing wins in every tournament in which women were allowed to play. In fact, Babe was accomplished in just about every sport—basketball, track, baseball, swimming, diving, boxing, volleyball, handball, bowling, billiards, skating and cycling! Sadly, her life was cut short by cancer and she died at the age of 45.

☆ TREMENDOUS TEXAS ☆

61. The east Texas town of Crockett is named after Davy Crockett, hero of the Alamo. Nearby you will find the Davy Crockett Memorial Park and Davy Crockett National Forest. Tradition says Crockett once camped in this area while on his way to the Alamo in 1836.

62. In 1981 Abilene held its centennial celebration. To mark the occasion, the city erected a drilling rig in order to demonstrate the oil drilling process. To everyone's surprise, the rig actually struck oil and the well sustained a modest production! Talk about dumb luck...

63. The pecan tree is the official state tree of Texas. A member of the hickory family, it produces an edible nut and useful wood. It is a large tree that grows as tall as 150 feet. It flowers in the spring and produces fruit (the pecans) in the fall.

64. Paint Rock, in west Texas, took its name from the extensive Indian pictographs painted on its limestone cliffs bordering the Concho River. The earliest of these paintings date from prehistoric times, with additional pictographs continuing until the last quarter of the 19th century when Comanche Indians still hunted in the area.

65. Originating in the 1820s as a volunteer corps to prevent Native American attacks, the Texas Rangers' exploits have become legendary. The Texas Rangers Hall of Fame Museum in Waco chronicles these famed lawmen who helped to tame the West. They exist today as a branch of the Texas Department of Public Safety.

66. Stephen F. Austin (1793-1836) is often referred to as the "Father of Texas." He was responsible for encouraging 1,200 settlers to make Mexican Texas their home.

67. Acton State Historic Site near Granbury claims to be Texas' smallest state park. At .01 acre, it's about the size of a standard two-car garage! It is the gravesite of Elizabeth Crockett, Davy Crockett's second wife. She was given the land by grant because of her husband's heroic actions at the Alamo. A monument was erected in 1914 and the area was declared a state park in 1949.

68. For the longest, narrowest state park, take a ride on the Texas State Railroad. The route is over 25.5 miles long and the width of the railway right-of-way! It runs between Palestine and Rusk.

69. The Lone Star flag became the official flag of Texas in 1933. The blue stands for loyalty, the white for strength and the red represents bravery. The single star on the Texas flag became the symbol and nickname of the Lone Star State.

☆ TREMENDOUS TEXAS ☆

70. Texas ranks number one in the U.S. in production of oil, natural gas, cattle, sheep, wool, rice, watermelon and cotton.

71. The Heisman Trophy is named for John William Heisman, first full-time coach and athletic director of Rice University in Houston.

72. The Dallas/Fort Worth Airport claims to have the world's largest parking lot!! With an airport larger than the size of Manhattan Island in New York City, valet parking sounds like the way to go!

73. The Dallas Arboretum and Botanical Garden showcases 30 species of ferns and 66 acres of blooming plants at its location on Garland Road. On its grounds is a spectacularly ornate mansion built in 1940 by oilman Everett DeGolyer. The 21,000 square foot house is definitely Texas-sized!

74. Quanah Parker, son of a Comanche chief and a captured white girl, was the last chief of the Comanches. He never lost a battle to the white man. He voluntarily surrendered his tribe in the mid-1870s only when he saw that there was no other alternative. He learned English, became a reservation judge, lobbied Congress and pleaded the cause of the Comanche Nation. Among his friends were cattleman Charles Goodnight and President Theodore Roosevelt.

75. The Blue Bell Creameries of Washington County produce about 20,000,000 gallons of ice cream each year. Quite an increase from its beginnings in 1911 when they produced two gallons a day!

76. Texas has produced some of the best golfers in the history of the game: Byron Nelson, Ben Hogan, Lee Trevino, Ben Crenshaw and Tom Kite.

77. Denison's claim to fame is being the birthplace of the 34th president, Dwight D. Eisenhower.

78. At 5,050 feet above sea level, the town of Fort Davis in west Texas is the highest town in the state. The town's slogan reads, "From Fort Davis, the rest of Texas is all downhill."

79. With all of the Army forts scattered throughout the state, it is not surprising that eight Texas towns begin with the word "Fort." They are Fort Clark Springs, Fort Davis, Fort Gates, Fort Griffin, Fort Hancock, Fort McKavett, Fort Stockton and Fort Worth.

80. In Eastland the United States Post Office has a 60 square foot stamp "mural" made up of 11,217 stamps! The Great Seal of the United States and a map of Texas are depicted.

☆ TREMENDOUS TEXAS ☆

81. Audie Murphy, the most decorated soldier of World War II, was born in Greenville. The public library displays artifacts from his war days; and, at Hill College, an entire museum honors his accomplishments (The Audie Murphy Memorial Gun Museum).

82. How's this for a Texas-sized bar? Billy Bob's in Fort Worth can hold 6,000 people and has 40 bars! It once served 16,000 bottles of beer in one night during a Hank Williams concert.

83. After winning the Battle of the Alamo in 1836, a Mexican colonel named Juan Almonte declared, "One more such glorious victory and we are finished." Little did he know, but six weeks later, his prediction would come true. The final battle of Texas' war for independence, the Battle of San Jacinto," was fought on April 21, 1836. And the rest, as they say, is history.

84. Texas' longest river is the Rio Grande. It flows through 1,270 miles of Texas and serves as the border between Texas and Mexico.

85. During World War II Sweetwater was the home of Avenger Field and the Women's Air Force Service Pilots (W.A.S.P.). Avenger Field, the first and only all-women military flying school in the world, trained female pilots for every kind of mission except combat. The W.A.S.P. flew 60 million miles on operational duty and thirty-eight of them died for their country.

86. Dallas began as a 640-acre claim laid out by Tennessee lawyer, John Neely Bryan, in 1841. He built a cabin and sketched out a town on the three forks of the Trinity River. President Polk's vice president, George Mifflin Dallas, was probably the city's namesake. Dallas ran on a platform favoring Texas statehood.

87. Galveston boasts a long list of Texas firsts: first post office (1836), first bakery (1838), first chapter of the Masonic Order (1840), first Catholic convent (1847) and first Cathedral (1847), first grocery store (1851), first private bank (1854), first opera house (1870), first electric lights (1883) and first country club (1898), among others.

88. Folks who like unexplained phenomena would enjoy a visit to Marfa. On clear nights, its Mystery Lights (also known as the Ghost Lights of Marfa) appear to be floating in the air. Some believe them to be UFOs, static electricity, reflections or swamp gas. Whatever they are, they continue to defy explanation and draw curious onlookers.

89. Texas leads the nation in cattle production with 14.8 million head. An additional 1.7 million head of sheep are raised each year as well.

☆ TREMENDOUS TEXAS ☆

90. In the bed of the Paluxy River at the Dinosaur Valley State Park exhibit near Glen Rose can be found the best dinosaur tracks ever preserved. Large, even by Texas standards, the prints tell an amazing story of the time when dinosaurs roamed this area 100 million years ago.

91. Alamo Village is actually a movie set that was constructed for the 1950s John Wayne movie, "The Alamo." Located in southwest Texas near Brackettville, visitors can tour a replica of the actual fort and 19th-century San Antonio. Among the largest sets ever built outside Hollywood, it is still used as a set for movies and commercials, most recently for the television series, "Lonesome Dove."

92. The King Ranch produced the first beef breed in the U.S. Called the Santa Gertrudis, it combines Indian Brahman cattle and British shorthorns.

93. Although "Remember the Alamo" is the battle cry most recollected, the war for independence also produced a lesser known appeal for revenge—"Remember Goliad." The Spanish presidio near Goliad was the scene of the execution of Colonel James Fannin and 340 of his men in 1836. Having surrendered to superior Mexican forces, they were later slaughtered by their captors. A monument dedicated to their memory now marks their common grave and the Fannin Battleground State Historical Park preserves the site of their fight and surrender.

94. Just north of Monahans lays Monahans Sandhills State Park. The park consists of 4,000 acres of sand and has been compared to the Sahara Desert. It has large wind swept dunes that rise as high as seventy feet and a forest of oak trees no taller than three feet high!

95. Mason County in central Texas is the site of what is left of old Fort Mason. The Officer's Quarters is a museum that has been reconstructed on the original foundation. Remaining foundations indicate where stables, storehouses, barracks, and the guardhouse once stood. Those who served at Fort Mason include George Armstrong Custer and General Albert Sidney Johnston, a Texas hero of the Civil War. General Robert E. Lee served his last assignment with the U.S. Army there before joining the Confederate forces.

96. The word "buckaroo" is actually a mispronunciation of the Spanish word "*vaqueros*" (wranglers) put into use by Texans who copied Mexican cattle-tending methods. Cowboys used a "lariat," "*la reata*," to catch calves.

97. Texas leads the nation in most farms (205,000) and most farmland (130,900,000 acres).

98. The Cowboy Artists' of America Museum in Kerrville preserves the life and customs of cowboys in paintings and bronzes. Here, kids are welcome to climb on saddles, touch a lasso and twirl a spur.

99. On January 10, 1901, Patillo Higgins and Anthony Lucas struck oil when they pierced a salt dome at Spindletop, east of Houston in Beaumont. Their rig produced 100,000 barrels of oil a day and close to 1,000,000 barrels spilled on the ground before the well was capped. It was then the richest discovery made in the U.S. and marked the beginning of the U.S. oil industry. The well itself dried up within 10 years.

100. Texas boasts 100 species of snakes, 16 of which are poisonous (southern copperhead, broad-banded copperhead, Trans-Pecos copperhead, Texas coral snake, western cottonmouth and 11 kinds of poisonous rattlesnakes).

☆ TREMENDOUS TEXAS ☆

101 The Sixth Floor Museum in Dallas' former Texas School Book Depository allows visitors to step back in time to November 22, 1963, the day President John F. Kennedy was shot there. Fascinating artifacts connected with the event are on display (like stills from the Zapruder movie) and you can look at the view sniper Lee Harvey Oswald had when he made history.

102. The Fort Worth Zoo is among the top zoos in the U.S. Its 5,000 inhabitants represent 709 species, 30 of which are endangered. Highlights include an 11-acre Texas area with native Texas animals and one of the largest reptile and amphibian collections in the nation.

103. The 570-foot San Jacinto Monument (15 feet higher than the Washington Monument) commemorates the battle that won Texas its independence from Mexico.

104. Twenty percent of all the Texas buildings listed on the National Register of Historic Places are in Waxahachie. Nicknamed the "Gingerbread City" because of the Victorian architecture of several of its home and buildings, 300 of the city's structures are listed on the Historic Register.

105. The falls that gave Wichita Falls its name were washed away in a flood in 1886. To mark their 100th anniversary, the townspeople rebuilt the falls. At 54 feet, they are now 10 times their original height and are built next to, not on, the Wichita River. Talk about fooling Mother Nature!

106. Twenty thousand items of circus memorabilia (including a model of a 1920s big top, posters and Tom Thumb items) are housed at the Hertzberg Circus Museum in San Antonio. Folks say it rivals the Ringling collection in Sarasota, Florida.

107. History claims that John Wilkes Booth, who assassinated President Lincoln, was killed by a search party while tracking down the murderer. But some believe that Booth escaped, ended up in Glen Rose, Texas and lived under the name of John St. Helen. It is reported that St. Helen confessed to killing Lincoln upon his deathbed. He later recovered and committed suicide. Witnesses who knew Booth confirmed that marks on St. Helen's body matched those on Booth's body.

108. Where can you find an orange house, orange sculpture, orange wishing wells, orange observation decks and lots of orange wheels? At Jeff McKissack's monument to his favorite fruit, the orange, in Houston. "Be smart; eat oranges" is spelled out in mosaic tiles.

109. Austin is considered the live music capital of the world.

110. Longhorn cattle were bred to be hardy beasts that could withstand the thousand mile drives to market, but would be a tough "chew" for today's consumer.

111. The only preserved battleship to see action in both world wars is docked near the San Jacinto Monument. The USS *Texas*, commissioned in 1914, is now undergoing long-term restoration. It is the state ship.

112. The Tyler Municipal Rose Garden claims to be the world's largest rose garden with 38,000 rose bushes. Five hundred varieties of roses are grown in its 22-acre garden. Tyler supplies 20% of the rose bushes sold in the U.S.

113. The Dallas-Fort Worth Airport lies almost entirely within the city limits of Grapevine.

114. Covering 500 acres and including more than 15 hospitals and medical and nursing schools, the Texas Medical Center in Houston is the world's largest medical complex. More than 125,000 people pass through it daily and it employs more than 51,000.

115. The Hilton Palacio del Rio Hotel in San Antonio was assembled in 1968 of 500 prefab, fully decorated cubes. Set in place by a crane, and built in a record 202 working days, each 35 ton, 900 square foot room unit was complete—down to ashtrays and bottle openers.

116. The "Big Ditch," a 432-mile section of the Gulf Intracoastal Waterway, provides a protected "superhighway" for shrimp boats, yachts and barges. The canal, completed in 1948, was built over a 44-year period. Barges move 75 million tons of goods through the Ditch each year.

117. The 70,504-acre Aransas National Wildlife Refuge is the winter home to North America's rare flock of whooping cranes. These endangered, 5-foot-tall birds (the tallest in North America), with wingspans of 7-1/2 feet, are studied by bird enthusiasts from all over the world.

118. Got a hankerin' for a Texas-sized steak? If you can eat a 72-ounce steak (that's 4-1/2 pounds!), shrimp cocktail, baked potato, salad and dinner roll in an hour (or less), the Big Texan Steak Ranch in Amarillo will give it to you for free!! Baseball player Frank Pastore who downed the dinner in nine minutes 45 seconds holds the record for fastest eater.

119. The town of Cut 'n Shoot, just east of Conroe, gets its name from the quote, "cut around the corner and shoot through the bushes."

120. Newspaper accounts say a Texan flew the first powered airplane in 1865—nearly 40 years before the Wright brothers (1903). Inventor/pilot Jacob Brodbeck reportedly reached treetop height with his coil-spring powered plane before crashing into a henhouse and killing several chickens.

121. The official state song is "*Texas, Our Texas,*" not "*The Eyes of Texas*" as many believe. It was written by composer William J. Marsh of Fort Worth with lyricist Gladys Yoakum Wright and adopted officially in 1929.

122. Each October the Confederate Air Force (formed in the 1950s to preserve World War II planes) recreates famous World War II air battles in its AirShow extravaganza. Its collection of 120 aircraft (Ghost Squadron) is housed at a museum in Midland.

☆ TREMENDOUS TEXAS ☆

123. At 6,791 feet, the highest point on any Texas highway, Mt. Locke provides an ideal spot for the University of Texas' McDonald Observatory. It is home to the Hobby-Eberly telescope, the third largest telescope in the world.

124. The Texas legislature, made up of 150 representatives and 31 senators, meets for 140 days every two years. Article VI, Section I, of their constitution denies the vote to idiots and lunatics!

125. Big Bend National Park is big even by Texas standards. At over 700,000 acres, the largest park in Texas includes forested Rio Grande flood plain, Chisos Mountains highlands, plunging canyons and hundreds of acres of Chihuahuan desert. A thousand plants, 450 bird species, 70 mammals, 115 types of butterflies, and 56 reptiles and amphibians live there.

126. The Texas state government is rather unique. The head of the executive branch is *nominally* the governor. The heads of several important state agencies are themselves directly elected and owe little or nothing to the governor. With rare exceptions, the governor is not allowed to dismiss or issue orders to any administrative personnel outside of his own staff. Almost all gubernatorial appointments require Senate confirmation. His influence is heavily dependent on political strength, the ability to shape public opinion and the capability to work effectively with the leadership of the legislature.

127. The lieutenant governor is the Senate's presiding officer, chosen by voters statewide. The members elect the speaker of the House of Representatives. Both have great power and influence in the legislative process.

128. An 18-foot floral clock welcomes over 600,000 visitors each year to the Fort Worth Botanic Garden. The garden also features a Fragrance Garden where the visually impaired (and sighted visitors) can enjoy touching and smelling the plants.

129. Here's an unusual collector's item—windmills! Windmill enthusiast Billie Wolfe gathered 170 of them and showcases them at the American Wind Power Center in Lubbock.

130. At the world's largest rattlesnake roundup in Sweetwater, four to five tons of rattlesnakes are collected each year! Started as a way to control the abundant snake population, the roundup features snake-handling demonstrations, a rattlesnake eating contest and prizes for the largest and most Western diamondbacks caught.

131. Gene Autry, the original singing cowboy and star of more than 100 movies, was born in the north Texas town of Tioga. Probably best known for singing "*Back in the Saddle Again*" and "*Rudolph the Red-Nosed Reindeer*," he also owned the California Angels baseball team.

132. At the Armstrong Browning Library at Baylor University in Waco is the world's largest collection of materials related to the lives and works of Robert and Elizabeth Barrett Browning. Fifty-six wonderful stained glass windows illustrate their works.

133. The only palm tree native to Texas is the Sabal palm. They can reach 20 to 48 feet in height and have feathery crowns and thick, bristly trunks. The Audubon Society grows them and other endangered species in a sanctuary in Brownsville.

134. George Strake hit oil in Conroe on June 4, 1932 and started the Conroe Field—which is still in production today. Strake is considered Houston's first million-dollar oil man.

135. Hundreds of notable writers were born in Texas. Among them: Larry McMurtry, *Lonesome Dove*, Wichita Falls; Katherine Anne Porter, *Ship of Fools*, Indian Creek; Cormac McCarthy, *All the Pretty Horses*, El Paso; James Lee Burke, *Two for Texas*, Houston; and Molly Ivins, *Molly Ivins Can's Say That, Can She?*, Austin.

136. Believed to be the longest wooden trestle-type bridge in the United States, the four foot wide, 546 feet long bridge in Rusk was built in 1861 to enable folks to get across a boggy valley in rainy weather. Replaced in 1889, it lasted until the 1950s and was restored again in 1969.

137. Highland Park Village, completed in 1931, is America's first shopping center and prototype for shopping centers all over the country. This unique Mediterranean/Spanish-style development is still a retail center today.

138. Mother Neff State Park is the first official state park in Texas. Named after the mother of Governor Pat M. Neff, the park has expanded to 259 acres from the original six acres Isabella Eleanor Neff donated in 1916.

139. Claiming to be the largest caverns in Texas, the Natural Bridge Caverns have been forming over the last 140 million years or so. Named for the 60-foot natural limestone bridge that spans its entrance, formations are still growing at an incredible cubic inch every 100 years.

140. The George Bush Presidential Library and Museum in College Station features a World War II Avenger torpedo bomber, a 1947 Studebaker, a slab of the Berlin Wall and precise replicas of former President Bush's Camp David and Air Force One offices. It has 36,000,000 pages of official and personal papers, more than 1,000,000 audiovisual records and 40,000 artifacts of his political career.

141. The Strecker Museum in Waco is the oldest continually operating museum in Texas. It houses an impressive collection of rocks, minerals, fossils, plants and animals from the area, as well as information about early man in central Texas. The museum had been instrumental in the discovery and preservation of Waco's mammoth site, finding remains of 23 of the beasts to date.

142. Believe it or not...According to apparently authentic records and witnesses, a Texas horned toad was sealed in the cornerstone of an Eastland courthouse in 1897. In 1928, when the old courthouse was demolished to build a new one, the cornerstone was opened to reveal a live horned toad! Named "Old Rip," after Rip Van Winkle, the animal became an instant celebrity and was exhibited nationally. When he <u>really</u> died the next year, Old Rip was embalmed and is still on view in a glass-front casket at the present courthouse.

143. The final battle for Texas' independence was fought on April 21, 1836 at San Jacinto outside of Houston. General Sam Houston surprised and overpowered Santa Anna's troops. The losses were 630 Mexican soldiers and nine Texan soldiers.

144. Probably the most famous spot in Texas is the Alamo where most of its 189 defenders were killed by Mexican troops led by General Antonio Lopez de Santa Anna. Santa Anna's troops pounded the fort for 13 days before taking it on March 16, 1836. Mexican losses were estimated at anywhere from 1,000 to 2,000 men. Today the Daughters of the Republic of Texas operate the Alamo as a shrine.

145. Perhaps the world's richest acre was located in Kilgore. In the 1930s more than 1,000 oil wells were located in downtown Kilgore, with 24 of them crammed into just over an acre of land.

146. Speaking of Kilgore, it's also the home to the Kilgore College Rangerettes who were the first to bring "show business" to football games with their precision high kicks and dances.

☆ TREMENDOUS TEXAS ☆

147. The largest cattle auction in Texas is held at Western Stockyards in Amarillo. They sell over 600,000 head of cattle annually.

148. The city of Texarkana is half in Texas and half in Arkansas. The Bi-State Justice Center houses courts and jails for both cities. The shared Post Office and Federal Building has the state line running down the middle of it. The building itself is constructed of Texas pink granite and Arkansas limestone.

149. The Odessa Meteor Crater, at 550 feet in diameter, is the second largest landmark of its kind in the U.S. It was probably created 20,000 to 30,000 years ago.

150. Texas ranks first in the U.S. in highway mileage, with over 70,000 miles.

151. Odessa has the world's largest jackrabbit statue, which stands 10 feet tall. They may be trying to outdo the nearby oversized statue of a roadrunner (Paisano Pete) in Fort Stockton.

152. Pecos is the birthplace of the rodeo and the legend of Pecos Bill, the roughest, toughest cowboy who never rode.

153. Freshwater pearls produced by a mussel in the Concho River are prized for their luster and beautiful pastel colors. Legend has it that several pieces of the crown jewels in Spain contain Concho pearls.

154. The world's largest statue of an American hero is the 67-foot figure of Sam Houston located in Huntsville. Houston called Huntsville home and it honors him with a 15-acre park and museum there.

☆ TREMENDOUS TEXAS ☆

155. Huntsville is also the site of the oldest prison in Texas, "The Walls." At the Texas Prison Museum you can see "Old Sparky," the infamous electric chair that electrocuted 361 inmates in its 40 years of operation.

156. For over 100 years, the Collin Street Bakery in Corsicana has been baking its world famous fruit-cake. It even won a Culinary Merit Award from the Gourmet Society.

157. In continuous operation since 1858, the Excelsior Hotel in Jefferson is the second oldest hotel in Texas—old enough to have had Ulysses S. Grant, Rutherford B. Hayes and Oscar Wilde as guests.

158. An average of 123 tornados touch down in Texas each year. From 1951 to 1993, 5,281 tornados were recorded.

159. Palo Duro Canyon is the largest and best known of a series of canyons in the Texas panhandle. It is 120 miles long and 20 miles wide at its widest point, and reaches down more than 1,100 feet. Geologists say you can step back 90 million years as you descend into the canyon. Spectacular views are best experienced in early morning and late evening.

160. Gonzales has been called the "Lexington of Texas," being the site of the first shot of the war for Texas' independence from Mexico. Ironically, that shot was fired from a cannon the Mexicans had loaned to the town's settlers to scare off threatening Indians.

161. Two of the three largest universities in the U.S. are in Texas: Texas A & M in College Station and the University of Texas at Austin.

☆ TREMENDOUS TEXAS ☆

162. Sam Rayburn began his illustrious political career in Bonham when he was elected to the Texas House of Representatives in 1906. "Mr. Sam," as he was affectionately known, went on to the U.S. House and served for 25 consecutive terms. He was Speaker of the House longer than any other man. His home is maintained as a museum in Bonham.

163. You don't have to cross the ocean to enjoy a bit of the "old bard." Odessa's Globe Theatre is a nearly authentic replica of the home of Shakespeare's acting company, originating in London. Performances are held year round, with a Shakespearean Festival each spring. A reproduction of Anne Hathaway's cottage is there, too.

164. Average annual precipitation ranges from 60 inches at Caddo Lake to 8.8 inches in El Paso.

165. Whether fact or fiction, the exploits of "Hanging Judge Roy Bean," who operated as "The Law West of the Pecos" in the town of Langtry, are the stuff of legends. When the Texas Rangers and railroad people appointed him Justice of the Peace, he presided over the frontier from his combination courthouse, saloon and pool hall. Bean often fined the guilty a $30 to $45 fine and ordered the rascal to buy a round of drinks for everyone in the court! He is reputed to have kept a bear in his courtroom and sentenced dozens to the gallows, saying "Hang 'em first, try 'em later."

166. The flagship location of upscale department store chain Neiman Marcus has been tempting shoppers in Dallas since 1907. Established by sister and brother Carrie Nieman and Herbert Marcus, their fifth floor exhibit tells the history of "The Store."

☆ TREMENDOUS TEXAS ☆

167. The Southfork Ranch in Plano was the exterior setting for the TV series "Dallas." A small museum there features memorabilia from the show for die-hard fans.

168. Singer/songwriter Charles Hardin ("Buddy") Holly was born in Lubbock on September 7, 1936. As a legendary rock pioneer, his impact on music can still be felt today. The Walk of Fame in Lubbock honors him and other west Texans who have made a significant contribution to the entertainment industry, including Waylon Jennings, Mac Davis and Jimmy Dean. An oversized bronze statue of Holly offers fans a unique photo op with the music "giant."

169. There are 6,736 lakes in Texas, giving it 4,959 square miles of inland water, first in the contiguous 48 states. Sounds like a lotta good fishin'...

170. Ever wanted to have your own castle? Sandy Feet and Amazin' Walter will help you build one out of sand on South Padre Island! These two professional sand castle builders have carved out a lucrative business there showing visitors how to construct eight-foot palaces, complete with towers and moats.

171. James Bowie, one of the heroes of the Alamo, was born in Kentucky. Known for his famous "Bowie Knife," Bowie searched for gold and silver in interior Texas. By some accounts, he is said to have found the fabled San Saba mines. He and William Travis shared authority during much of the siege of the Alamo, but pneumonia disabled Bowie and he was confined to his cot when the fort fell.

172. Texas was the 28th state to join the Union on December 29, 1845.

173. Texas has 91 mountains over a mile in elevation, all in the far west region. Guadalupe Peak is the state's highest at 8,749 feet and can be found at Guadalupe Mountains National Park. Created in 1972, it is one of Texas' newest parks.

174. The largest military base in the world is Fort Hood, located in Killeen.

175. In the category of creepy plants, pitcher plants certainly stand out. Found in the swampy, bug-infested lowlands of east Texas, they are distinguished by big green flowers with red and purple veins called "pitchers" on top. They give off an odor that attracts insects that are devoured when they wander too close!

176. El Paso claims to be the first place margaritas were served.

177. Padre Island is the longest, undeveloped barrier island in the world. It stretches for 110 miles along the Texas Gulf Coast. It was named for Padre Jose Nicolas Balli who built a mission there in the 1800s to bring Christianity to the native Karankawa Indians.

178. The Karankawas, as reported by Spanish settlers, painted their faces yellow and blue and pierced their nipples and lower lips. They also smeared their bodies with mud and animal fats to repel mosquitoes. Adding further to their fierce aura, they reportedly ate parts of their dead enemies, as well as parts of <u>living</u> prisoners. They were eventually displaced from their ancestral lands and moved to west Texas where they are thought to have died out.

179. "Houston" was the first word spoken from the surface of the moon in 1969.

180. The Big Thicket National Preserve, covering 5,469 square miles north and west of Beaumont, is unique not just for its unusual plant and animal life, but for the variety of ecosystems found there. Its dense foliage once offered a perfect refuge for outlaws, runaway slaves and gamblers. (If you're fascinated by those pitcher plants, they have a hiking trail that takes you by four of the five species of meat-eating plants found in the Preserve.)

181. Amistad National Recreation Area was created in the late 1960s when a dam and reservoir transformed 105 square miles of the Rio Grande. It spans the U.S. and Mexico with 547 miles of shoreline in the U.S. and 304 in Mexico. Indians who lived in this area left behind a wealth of rock art that can be still be seen today.

182. Four national forests are found in east Texas. They were established primarily for forestry purposes, but recreational opportunities abound at each of them, too. Angelina National Forest is the smallest at 239 square miles. It contains the Sam Rayburn Reservoir and offers hiking, boating and fishing. Davy Crockett National Forest, at 251 square miles, is one of the less developed forests. It offers canoeing and hiking. Sabine National Forest is 251 square miles. Visitors can boat, camp and hike there. Sam Houston National Forest is the largest at 255 square miles and visitors can enjoy its mountain bike trails, swimming, canoeing and hiking.

183. Lake Meredith National Recreational Area, the result of the Sanford Dam on the Canadian River, was created mainly to supply water to arid panhandle towns. It is a popular boating and fishing area.

184. Alibates Flint Quarries National Monument commemorates the importance of flint. Early inhabitants mined this area for thousands of years and used the flint for tools, weapons and an early form of currency. Besides the actual quarries, visitors can see what's left of the villages built by the flint miners.

185. Not only do birds flock to the South in the winter months, but so do 100,000 or so retired folks, affectionately known as Winter Texans. There are scores of senior citizen RV and mobile home parks from Brownsville to McAllen that welcome these folks to their communities as volunteers and thrifty shoppers. They reportedly add $250 million to the Texas economy each winter.

186. Workers in the oil fields were known in their trade as "rough-necks."

187. El Paso was the epitome of the Wild West. Billy the Kid, Wyatt Earp, Bat Masterson and John Wesley Hardin all played a part in the city's colorful history. Hardin, the fastest gun of them all, claimed to have killed 40 men before being killed there in 1895.

188. Fort Bliss is the largest air defense training center in the Western world. Military personnel from approximately 25 allied nations train here. Its 1.2 million acre reservation makes it one of the largest military installations in Texas.

189. Fifty rooms of exhibits offer something for everyone at the West of the Pecos Museum in Pecos. Once a saloon and hotel, this museum preserves the colorful frontier history of the area. The rooms depict local life ranging from pioneer homes to the elected Queens of the Rodeo.

190. Terlingua is best known as the home of the Chili Cook-Off. There are actually two rival cook-offs, drawing 10,000 people to the town each November.

191. Dallas hosts the largest state fair in the U.S. with attendance well over 3,000,000. Big Tex, a cowboy with a five-foot, 75-gallon hat, greets visitors at the gate.

192. On September 8, 1863, a Union fleet of about 20 ships and several thousand men tried to invade Texas through Sabine Pass. Keeping them at bay was a young lieutenant, Dick Dowling, and some 40 Irish dockworkers with six cannons. In an hour, Dowling and his men had overcome two gunboats, killed or wounded 65 Union soldiers and captured 315 of them, while not losing a man or cannon.

193. The Mesquite Rodeo has become the best-known rodeo in the country with attendance of about 300,000 a season. Every Friday and Saturday night the traditional cowboy competitions begin and the 6,000-seat arena fills with excited fans. Ride 'em, cowboy!

194. Dominique de Menil funded not only one of the finest small museums in the nation, but also worked to desegregate Houston and highlight human rights abuses worldwide. A variety of art and periods are represented in the Menil Collection, housed in a building that is a work of art in itself.

195. Attention, dog lovers. You can visit a cemetery devoted to Texas' all-time great foxhounds at Boles Field in Center. Interment ceremonies include hunting stories about these beloved working hounds.

196. The Caddoan Indian Mounds in Alto provide a glimpse of the most sophisticated prehistoric Indian culture in Texas. Archaeologists think that the mounds here are dated from about 780 to 1200 AD.

197. Spur 94 is the shortest highway in the state. The two-block long road takes you to Sam Houston's grave and monument.

198. Marshall Pottery is Texas' oldest potter, established in 1896, and the largest manufacturer of red clay pots in America.

199. Davy Crockett slept here. In Paris, that is. Female outlaw Belle Starr was locked up in its jail. Frank James was a clerk in a Paris dry goods store; and John Chisum, a cattleman of the 1800s, lived and is buried there.

☆ TREMENDOUS TEXAS ☆

200. Tol Barret drilled the first oil well in Texas, just after the Civil War, in Nacogdoches. It only produced ten barrels, so it was quickly abandoned.

201. The Lyndon B. Johnson Library sits on a knoll overlooking the University of Texas in Austin. There are four stories worth of presidential papers and other memorabilia packed in this site.

202. Finished in 1856, the Governor's mansion is still in use today. Originally built for $17,000, its first inhabitant, Governor Elisha Pease, had to bring his own furnishings with him!

203. As Secretary of War, Jefferson Davis established a U.S. Army camel corps at Camp Verde in 1856. It was thought that camels would be a dependable means of transportation in the semiarid plains. Apparently not.

204. The Bastrop family was important in Texas history. Three Bastrop men signed the Texas Declaration of Independence, 11 died at the battle of the Alamo and 60 or so lost their lives at San Jacinto.

205. Hico residents insist that Billy the Kid wasn't killed by Pat Garrett in New Mexico, but lived under the alias of Brushy Bill Roberts in their town until 1950, when he succumbed to a heart attack at age 92.

206. La Grange can boast of several firsts: the first Protestant College in the Republic (Rutersville College, 1840); the first rural free delivery (RFD) in Texas (1889); and the first roadside park (1933). It's also home to the "Chicken Ranch" of *Best Little Whorehouse in Texas* fame.

207. Topaz, the Texas gemstone, is found in abundance in Mason. One topaz crystal found there weighed 1,296 grams (almost three pounds) and is exhibited at the Smithsonian Museum in Washington, D.C.

208. Teddy Roosevelt trained his Rough Riders in San Antonio.

209. Bill Pickett, a black cowboy born in 1870 in Taylor, is credited with creating the rodeo event known as "bulldogging." He would gain control of a steer by sinking his teeth into its upper lip and hanging on like a bulldog as he twisted the steer's neck and brought it down.

210. The tallest Ferris wheel in North America is the 212-foot (20 story high) ride at Fair Park. It was originally built in Italy.

211. All in the family...When Governor James E. ("Pa") Ferguson was impeached and removed from office in 1917, he ran his wife, Miriam A. ("Ma") Ferguson in his place. She became the first woman governor in Texas. Her campaign slogan? "Two governors for the price of one."

212. John Nance Garner, Uvalde's famous son, served as a U.S. congressman from 1903-1933 when he began two terms as vice president for FDR. "Cactus Jack," as he was called, is quoted as saying that the position of vice president "isn't worth a bucket of warm spit."

213. Fair Park in Dallas, built for the Texas Centennial in 1936, is still in use today. It not only serves as the site of the annual State Fair; but also is the location of several museums, historic places and entertainment and sports events.

214. The prestigious Van Cliburn International Piano Competition is held every four years in Fort Worth. The next competition, the twelfth, will he held in 2005.

215. You can touch a moon rock, walk through Skylab and imagine what it's like to fly in space at the NASA/Lyndon B. Johnson Space Center in Houston.

216. At the Texas State Aquarium in Corpus Christi, interactive exhibits allow visitors to view ecosystems of the Gulf of Mexico and the Caribbean.

217. Laredo was the capital of the independent Republic of Rio Grande for a total of 283 days in 1840. The Mexican Army quashed the rebellion on day 284.

218. A 14-foot high, 2.5-mile long seawall, designed by sculptor Gutzon Borglum (creator of Mt. Rushmore), was completed in 1941 in Corpus Christi. It steps down into the bay and provides a great place to walk, jog, skate, cycle or lunch while in the city.

219. In the 1880s, the XIT Ranch in Dalhart was the largest ranch in the world under a single fence. Its 3,000,000 acres of land were corralled by a fence that stretched for 6,000 miles. It was created by northern investers who were contracted to build the capitol building in Austin. The XIT Museum in town tells the ranch's colorful history and displays memorabilia of its grand days.

220. Spanning the Laguna Madre Bay is Texas' longest bridge, the Queen Isabella Causeway, measuring 2.6 miles.

221. Ninety percent of the world's supply of helium is found in reserves in Amarillo and the adjacent area.

222. Outside Amarillo is Cal Farley's Boys Ranch. Established in 1939 by prizefighter Farley, the ranch provides a home for more than 400 orphaned and troubled boys.

223. The state's oldest identifiable ethnic group is the Tigua Indians. Today, more than 600 of them are connected with the Tigua Indian Reservation in El Paso. They operate a living history pueblo and casino at the site.

224. Some of the most important rock art in the New World can be seen at Fate Bell Shelter in Seminole Canyon State Historical Park. Experts think the images there were painted about 8,000 years ago.

225. In the Old West, to "Pecos" a man meant to kill him, weigh his body down with rocks and toss him in a river.

226. Amarillo is Spanish for "yellow," which refers to the area's characteristic yellow soil.

227. River Walk in San Antonio was the creation of the WPA. Begun in 1939 as a way to handle drainage problems of the San Antonio River, the canal area was developed into a central business district of shops and restaurants along a cobbled walk. It serves as an aesthetic and commercially viable area of the city today.

228. The temperature has reached the 120 degree mark on two different occasions. On August 12, 1936, the town of Seymour hit the high mark and on June 28, 1994 it was Odessa's time to sizzle.

229. In 1821, Jane Long, while waiting for her husband General James Long to return from Mexico, gave birth to the first Anglo-Saxon native Texan, Mary Jane Long, on Bolivar Peninsula. Jane is known as "The Mother of Texas."

230. The world's littlest skyscraper is found at 701 LaSalle in Wichita Falls. Planned in the early 20th century to be 120 feet tall, it was built in inches—not feet—and bilked investors out of hundreds of thousands of dollars.

231. The longest highway in any one state is U.S. 83. It runs for 903 miles from Brownsville to the Panhandle.

232. Of the state's 29 coastal and inland water ports, the Port of Houston is the largest in size and is one of the three busiest ports in the United States.

233. Enchanted Rock, located north of Fredricksburg, is actually a massive dome of Precambrian pink granite covering 640 acres and rising 425 feet. Believed to be more than one <u>billion</u> years old, it's some of the oldest "rock" in North America. Indians worshiped it and believed evil spirits lived in it!

234. On Malone Street in Houston is a house constructed of 50,000 beer cans.

235. Southern Methodist University in Dallas is Texas' most expensive institute of higher learning. A benefactor donated 100 Spanish paintings by such artists as Goya, Velazquez and Miro.

236. Fort Worth's National Cowgirl Museum and Hall of Fame salutes not only women who worked on ranches, like Henrietta Chamberlin King (co-founder of the King Ranch), but also entertainers like TV's Dale Evans and Country/Western singer Patsy Cline.

237. Noted architect I. M. Pei, designer of the glass pyramid at the Louvre in Paris, also designed several buildings in Texas: City Hall in Dallas; the 60-story Wells Fargo building in Dallas; and the Texas Commerce Bank Building— nicknamed the "Texas Tombstone" because of its sleek, gray appearance— in Houston.

238. Houstonians reputedly eat out more than any other city in the U.S. at an average of 4.9 times per week. (Might be because they have so many choices—around 6,000 restaurants tempt Houston's citizens!)

239. At Arlington's Ballpark, no Texas Rangers' fan is farther than 75 feet from a TV monitor from which to watch the baseball game—even while buying a hotdog!

240. Vander Clyde, from Round Rock, became famous in the 1920s for his daring aerialist stunts in Paris.

241. Samuel Colt designed the gun that became the standard weapon of the Texas Rangers in the 1850s.

242. With a cast of 600, including Comanches and lots of Easter bunnies, the folk of Fredricksburg retell the story of the founding of their town each year before Easter. Somehow, Indian and German legends collided and Indian signal fires turned into fires to boil up Easter eggs by the Easter Bunny. It's a real "melting pot" of a drama at their Easter Fire Pageant!

243. Mirabeau B. Lamar, second president of the Republic of Texas, is called the "Father of Education in Texas."

244. Dr. Annie Webb Blanton became the first woman elected to statewide office in Texas when she won the race for State Superintendent of Public Instruction in 1918. Eight years later, Margie Neal of Carthage was elected the state's first woman senator.

245. During the Great Depression, the murals program of the U.S. government put needy artists to work painting murals around the country. More than 65 post offices in Texas were decorated with nearly 100 individual murals featuring scenes of local interest, history, folklore and industry. Most of these survive today.

246. The Angelina River was named for a Caddoan Indian woman whom the Spanish called Angelina, "little angel." A county and national forest are named for this river.

247. The Tarpon Inn in Port Aransas is listed on the National Register of Historic Places. Its lobby walls are covered with more than 7,000 autographed tarpon scales, including one signed by Franklin Roosevelt. Anglers used to leave a record of their prized catch by writing their name, hometown, date and size of the catch on a two to three inch tarpon scale that was then attached to the walls. Anglers used to come from all over the country to fish for tarpon, which are now scarce in these waters.

248. Women's Clubs founded eighty-five percent of the public libraries in Texas.

249. Port Arthur was the childhood home of Janis Joplin and football coach Jimmy Johnson. The "Big Bopper," Jiles Perry Richardson, Jr. of *"Chantilly Lace"* fame, also hailed from there.

250. Corn has been cultivated in Texas for at least 2,000 years.

251. The song, "*The Yellow Rose of Texas*," was written in 1836 around the time of the Battle of San Jacinto. Supposedly, the story is one of a black soldier who left his sweetheart and longs to return to her. "Yellow" was the term used to describe an American of mixed race and "Rose" was a popular 19th-century name. Hence the song title. Both the North and the South used it as a marching song during the Civil War.

252. Selena Quintanilla-Perez, who grew up in Corpus Christi, rose to the top of the Tejano music scene before her untimely death at age 23. Several buildings are named for her and a statue of her likeness can be found in Corpus Christi.

253. The Bois d'Arc Bayou, in Grayson and Fannin counties, was named after the tree of the same name by the French because the Indians favored its wood for making their bows.

254. Much of what we know about the early Indian tribes of southern Texas comes from the accounts of Cabeza de Vaca, a Spanish explorer who was shipwrecked on the Texas coast and explored the area from 1528 until 1536.

255. German traditions and cultures are strong in New Braunfels, which was settled by German immigrants in the 1850s. Their annual Wurstfest each fall draws over 100,000 visitors from all over the country. Most of the activities center around drinking beer, eating its famous sausage, dancing, singing and drinking more beer!

256. The state's first historic district is a 25-block area near downtown San Antonio known as the King William District. Prominent German merchants originally settled the area that became an elegant residential area by the late 1800s. Many of its restored homes are open for tourists to visit.

257. The monarch butterfly is the official state insect. This species does not hibernate, but migrates in changing seasons. Three to four generations of these beautiful black and orange butterflies are produced each year.

258. Who's calling? More than 55 percent of Southwestern Bell customers in the state have caller ID service, the highest percentage in the country. Houston's rate is 56 percent and Laredo tops out at 70 percent. The national average is about 30 percent.

259. George W. Bush, the 43rd President of the United States, was formerly the 46th Governor of the State of Texas. Born on July 6, 1946, he grew up in Midland and Houston. After graduating from college, he served as an F-102 pilot for the Texas Air National Guard. He went on to a career in the oil and gas industry in Midland, and later became a partner in the Texas Rangers baseball franchise. He was elected Governor on November 8, 1994, and re-elected in 1998, becoming the first Texas Governor to be elected to consecutive four-year terms.

260. George W. Bush (2001-present) and his father, George Bush (1989-93), are the second father and son to both serve as U.S. Presidents. John Adams (1797-1801) and his son, John Qunicy Adams (1825-29), were the first to do so.

261. In Corpus Christi, you can find authentic seaworthy replicas of the Nina, Pinta and Santa Maria, Christopher Columbus' sailing ships.

262. Mrs. Lyndon Baines Johnson was born Claudia Alta Taylor in Karnack on December 22, 1912. Her nursemaid once remarked that she was "as purty as a lady bird," and the nickname "Lady Bird" was born. Her interest in environmentalism led her to get thousands of tulips and daffodils planted in Washington, D.C when she was the First Lady. And the Highway Beautification Act of 1965 was the result of her national campaign for beautification.

263. With an estimated 678,000 horses in Texas, or nearly 10 percent of the country's horse population, Texas ranks No. 1 in the U.S. in horses.

264. Texas also ranks No. 1 in the number of registered quarter horses—with around 450,000.

265. Texans spend more money on hunting than any
other state, according to the U.S. Department of
Interior's Fish and Wildlife Service.

266. The state fruit is the "Texas Red Grapefruit."

267. The largest bass caught in the state is an 18-
pound, four-ounce whopper reeled in by Barry
St. Clair from Lake Fork in 1992. Texas has officially logged five bass in the 17-pound class, all
caught from Fork.

268. The lightening whelk is the state shell, named for
its colored stripes. Found only along the Gulf
Coast, it is one of the few shells that has its aper-
ture on the left side.

269. Popeye would love it in Texas. The state ranks first in the amount of spinach grown for processing. In fact, there is a statue of the cartoon sailor in Crystal City, the spinach capital of the U.S.

270. Harmon A. Dobson, a Corpus Christi entrepreneur, founded the Whataburger chain in 1950. Anxious to give the customer a choice of what was on his burger, Dobson created his idea of the ultimate burger: a grilled quarter-pound 100% beef patty on a five inch bun with choice of lettuce, tomato, dill pickle, onion, mustard, salad dressing or ketchup. The Whataburger's distinctive orange and white striped roof on an A-frame building can be found throughout the Sunbelt.

271. Houston has been called the "Egg Roll Capital of the World," rolling out around 750,000 of the tasty, oriental tidbits *every day* from two plants in the city.

272. Texas is a favorite spot for migrating birds. According to the Parks and Wildlife Department, 618 different species (the largest number of any state) have been seen and recorded in here.

273. Texans love their barbeque and can find it at 929 establishments statewide. Houston alone has 103 barbeque restaurants—more than any of the nation's top ten cities.

274. Llano boasts of being the "Deer Capital of the World," having the highest concentration of deer in the U.S. It's also considered as one of the best places in the state for bow-hunting.

275. Llano County is the only place in the world where the unusual mineral, llanite, can be found. It is a rare type of brown granite embedded with crystals of pink and blue feldspar.

276. Texas was the only state to put the issue of secession to a statewide vote. After its citizens voted overwhelmingly in favor of the move, Texas seceded from the Union and joined the Confederacy in 1861.

277. Austin is proud to boast that William Sydney Porter, better known as short story master O. Henry, once lived there. The O. Henry Museum in town sponsors a "Pun Off" competition annually in May.

278. Kimble County is a leading producer of wool and mohair. Angora goats were introduced in Texas in 1849, and Texas has produced the most mohair in the country since the 1920s.

279. The Karankawa Indians were expert marksmen, able to fell prey from 100 yards with cedar bows.

280. Central Texas has more than its share of bats and Mason ranks right up there with Austin in this regard. An enormous colony of Mexican free-tailed bats summers there each year. Their spectacular exodus and returning flights can be observed at the Eckert James River Bat Preserve from May to October.

281. Spanish explorer Alonzo Alvarez Pineda is generally credited with the discovery of the Coastal Bend, the area around Corpus Christi, while on a 1519 voyage to find the Spice Islands of the Pacific. He is also credited with discovering the Mississippi River and is said to have named the Corpus Christi Bay after the Roman Catholic Feast of Corpus Christi.

282. Onions are the Lone Star State's leading vegetable crop with sales reaching $100 million per year.

283. Speaking of onions, Dr. Leonard Pike developed one of the nation's most famous sweet onions, the Texas 1015Y. It gets its name from its ideal planting date, October 15. It also has the distinction of being the state vegetable.

284. While in Texas, you're likely to hear Mexican-American music of various types: *Mariachi*, typically includes one or more trumpets, violins, a *vihuela* (a five-stringed instrument), guitars, harp and a *guitarron* (a six-string bass guitar). They usually play a *ranchera,* a bluesy ballad, but you might hear a polka, *cumbias* and *boleros. Tejano* is a mix of traditional Mexican polkas, *cumbias* and *rancheras*, updated with American blues, pop and country strains. *Conjunto* is an accordion-type folk music handed down from the German and Czech immigrants who settled Texas.

☆ TREMENDOUS TEXAS ☆

285. You can find Utopia on earth—in Texas, as a matter of fact. Originally the town had several other names until a postmaster, having read Sir Thomas More's idea of Utopia: "Perfect climate, happy, healthy people…," decided that it was a perfect description of his town!

286. The First State Bank of Uvalde houses the extensive art collection of former Governor and Mrs. Dolph Briscoe. Everything from Rembrandt etchings of 1633 to works of Gainsborough, Reynolds and Western artists can be seen here.

287. There are more tortilla plants in Texas than anywhere else in the country, with 70 factories shipping product all over the world.

288. The National Polka Festival is held in Ennis every Memorial Day Weekend celebrating its Czech roots.

289. The Texas Bluebonnet Tartan was conceived and designed by June P. McRoberts, using the colors and symmetry of the state flower. It was officially registered with the Scottish Tartan Society Museum in Scotland and adopted as the Sesquicentennial Tartan in 1986.

290. During the Great Depression East Texans stocked their larders with armadillos. They called them "Hoover hogs" because of the animal's supposed pork-like taste (some would argue chicken-like!) and because they felt President Hoover was responsible for the Depression.

291. The Texas palm, or Texas palmetto, which reaches a height of 50 feet, has a large trunk and fan-shaped leaves that form a rounded crown. As the leaves die, they fall toward the trunk where they cling, unless trimmed away. Texas palms are a common landscape shrub in southern Texas.

292. Dallas has more shopping centers per capita than any other major U.S. city and it has the world's largest wholesale trade complex (Dallas Market Center).

293. Texas has about 11,500 historical markers. More than 700 local history museums, 40,000 recorded archeological sites and more than 2,000 other sites are listed in the National Register of Historic Places.

294. Texas leads the nation in the sale of pick-up trucks.

295. "Empressarios" were people who contracted with the Mexican government to bring Roman Catholic settlers to Texas in exchange for 23,000 acres of land for each 100 families. Stephen Austin was considered an empressario.

296. Huge herds of cattle were slaughtered in Rockport after the Civil War to provide Easterners with hides for leather goods, tallow for candles and soap, bones for fertilizer and horns for buttons and combs. Meat was considered a side-product and much of it was thrown away.

297. Each summer endangered Kemp's ridley sea turtle hatchlings are released into the wild at the Padre Island National Seashore in an effort to expand their nesting grounds and increase their chance of survival.

298. *"The Eyes of Texas"* is the official song of the University of Texas at Austin. Many consider it an unofficial state song. It is sung by coaches, players and fans alike following every sporting event, whether football, swimming, golf or badminton.

299. Aransas Pass refers to itself as the "shrimping capital of Texas." It has the largest fleet of shrimp trawlers on the Gulf Coast.

300. Almost 400 wildflowers are known to bloom in Texas. With the help of Lady Bird Johnson, wildflower enthusiasts founded the National Wildflower Research Center in Austin. They plant wildflowers along public roads.

301. In the unusual fauna category is the distinctive-looking javelina that roams the Aransas National Wildlife Refuge. A javelina is a gregarious, American mammal (also known as the collared peccary) that looks like a wild pig.

302. The mesquite tree that dots South Texas actually provided a beverage for desperate early settlers. They reportedly dried and roasted the tree's beans to make a bitter sort of coffee.

303. Mesquite reproduces easily, making it a good source of wood for flavoring barbeques, a good producer of blossoms for honey and a shady refuge for cows and deer.

304. Converse, northeast of San Antonio, has the oldest 4-H Club in Texas.

305. The late birder and researcher Roger Tory Peterson published 34 birding guidebooks. Texas was the only state that merited its own book, Peterson's *Field Guide to the Birds of Texas*, because of the diversity of its bird population.

306. Mustang Island was first called Wild Horse Island because of the wild horses called Mestenos that used to roam its shores. The Spanish introduced the horses in the 1800s.

307. Sometimes called the "Billion Dollar House," Pompeiian Villa was built in Port Arthur in 1900 for "Barbed-Wire King" Isaac Ellwood. He soon sold it to matchstick mogul James Hopkins of the Diamond Match Company. Unfortunately Hopkins' wife didn't like the area, so he traded it to George Craig, banker, for $10,000 in shares of a new oil company, Texas Company (which became Texaco). That stock would be worth more than a billion dollars today. The home was modeled after a villa uncovered in Pompeii and is listed on the National Register of Historic Places.

308. The Texas Rangers, a major league baseball team, was established in the Dallas-Fort Worth area in 1972. Baseball great Ted Williams was its first manager. Their Ballpark in Arlington was opened in 1994.

309. Well-preserved woven sandals, made by prehistoric people in Texas, have been found by archeologists in the dry rock shelters in southwestern areas of the state.

310. Into creepy crawlers? Texas grows 'em big! A species of giant roach, also known as a "tree roach," can grow up to three inches in length and an inch or so wide!

311. Bonnie Parker (of Bonnie and Clyde) was an honor student in Dallas before becoming one of the country's most infamous criminals.

312. West Texas was one of the first wine-producing areas in the U.S. In 1662, a century before vines were planted in California, Franciscan padres from Mexico established vineyards in the El Paso area to produce sacramental wine.

313. Wink has a museum devoted to the memorabilia of native son and rock 'n roll legend Roy Orbison who sang such hits as *"Pretty Woman"* and *"Only the Lonely."*

314. The east Texas town of Athens holds two distinctions. First, it's known as the "Black-Eyed Pea Capital of the World" and celebrates the legume at a jamboree each year. Second, it's recognized as the birthplace of the hamburger. In the late 1880s café owner Fletcher Davis created the first hamburger sandwich. He even took it to the 1904 St. Louis World's Fair.

315. Texas had a nine-hole golf course in 1886 and an exhibition game was played there in 1887. The Texas Golf Hall of Fame outside of Houston is a treasure trove for golf history buffs.

316. Fred Gipson, author of *Old Yeller*, was born in Mason.

317. The McAllen area claims to be the "Square Dance Capital of the World" because of the number of dancers and dances, callers and dance cuers who either live in the valley or winter there. Each February around 2,000 dancers do-se-do at the annual Texas Square Dance Jamboree.

318. The Val Verde Winery is Texas' oldest. Begun in 1883 by Italian immigrant Frank Qualia, it is still owned by the family and producing wine.

319. NASCAR's Texas Motor Speedway, which opened in Fort Worth in 1997, seats 150,061, making it the second-largest sports facility in the U.S.

☆ TREMENDOUS TEXAS ☆

320. The father of Texas, Stephen F. Austin's middle name was Fuller.

321. Barbara Jordan was the first African-American elected to the Texas Senate in 1966.

322. Ann Richards became the first woman Governor of Texas in 1990.

323. The Camino Real Paso Del Norte Hotel in El Paso has a Tiffany glass dome in its elegant Dome Bar. Built in 1912, the hotel's guests have included Pancho Villa, President Taft and Colonel "Blackjack" Pershing. It is listed on the National Register of Historic Places.

324. Historic Fort Concho was the home of the heroic Buffalo Soldiers, black troops named in admiration by their Native American enemies.

325. Spanning nearly two acres is the world's largest spring-fed swimming pool in Balmorhea State Park near Fort Davis. It is thirty feet deep and contains three and a half million gallons of water that stays a cool 72 to 76 degrees year round.

326. For over thirty summers, *TEXAS! A Musical Drama* has been entertaining visitors to the Palo Duro Canyon. Nearly 100,000 people have experienced the outdoor spectacle that tells the story of Panhandle pioneers in song and dance.

327. Since the middle of the nineteenth century, folks have been coming to Canton for First Monday Trade Days. Actually held the Friday, Saturday and Sunday preceding the first Monday of the month, shoppers can find everything from clothes and farm equipment to Depression glass and quilts. With some 5,000 vendors, there's sure to be something for everyone!

328. The small town of Uncertain claims it got its name when it was contemplating incorporation. A poll of its citizens was taken to choose a town name and "Uncertain" was frequently listed on the third-choice line!

329. Feeling a bit tongue-tied? Maybe you need to kiss the Blarney Stone in Shamrock! County Cork (Ireland) shared a bit of their famous rock with the folks in Texas and promise the gift of eloquence to anyone who kisses it.

330. The Devil's Backbone is one of the state's most scenic drives, following a 25-mile wildly twisting Ranch Road 32 along a ridge from Wimberley south toward Blanco.

331. Clute, located on the coast, celebrates the Great Texas Mosquito Festival each July, paying tribute to Willie Manchew, "the world's largest mosquito."

☆ TREMENDOUS TEXAS ☆

332. The Bishop's Palace in Galveston is a grandiose home designed by architect Nicholas Clayton in the 1880s. It is listed as one of the hundred most architecturally significant buildings in the United States by the American Institute of Architects.

333. The Houston Texans football team played its debut game on September 8, 2002, beating the Dallas Cowboys 19 to 10.

334. Jefferson's Texas Heritage Archives and Library houses over 600 rare and historic maps of Texas, the Southwest and the New World. Its research library has the largest collection of Texas bank notes and land grants dating back to the first Anglo settlements.

335. The Inks Dam National Fish Hatchery's scientific ponds breed thousands of fish for stocking lakes across the country.

336. Made of eel, snakeskin, calfskin, lizard or other exotic leathers, a pair of world-renowned James Leddy cowboy boots will set you back $500 to $3500. The Abilene boot maker promises a pair of custom-made boots within two to three months.

337. The city of Wellington was named after England's Duke of Wellington. It was among the estates on the Rocking Chair Ranch more than a century ago. Also called Nobility Ranch by Texas cowboys, its owners were British noblemen, the Baron of Tweedsmouth and the Earl of Aberdeen.

338. Presbyterian-supported Austin College in Sherman was the state's first college to grant a graduate degree, the first to start a law school and the first to have a national fraternity. Sam Houston, one of its first trustees, gave them a bell that hangs in their chapel.

339. The Rainforest Pyramid in Moody Gardens in Galveston houses a 10-story, 40,000 square foot exhibit of exotic plants, birds, butterflies and fish in a tropical setting, complete with waterfalls, cliffs, wetlands and forests. You can also visit Bat Cave, the largest exhibit of its kind in the Southwest. There sure are a lot of bats in Texas!

340. The Pilgrims Pride poultry people produce over 600 million pounds of plucked poultry yearly in Pittsburg. Say that ten times fast!!

341. Going south on U.S. Route 83, you will eventually wind up at the Rio Grande River. For 25 cents you can ride the Los Ebaños Ferry across the Rio Grande to Mexico. It is a wooden, two-car ferry hand-pulled by a Mexican crew using ropes. You won't find another sight like this along the entire U.S. border!

☆ TREMENDOUS TEXAS ☆

342. The White Elephant Saloon in Fort Worth, a century-old barroom, was named "One of the Best 100 Bars in America" by *Esquire* magazine.

343. A life-sized statue of Peter Pan "flies" in front of the Weatherford Public Library. It honors famous "daughter" Mary Martin who originated the role of Peter Pan on Broadway.

344. Floydata in the Panhandle is known as the Pumpkin Capital of the U.S. Big Macs—the hundred-pound pumpkins grown there—are displayed at Punkin Days held every October right before Halloween. Try your hand at pumpkin bowling or a seed-spitting contest!

345. The Houston Fire Museum showcases not only the history of the Houston Fire Department, but also displays paraphernalia, photos and period uniforms from fire-fighting units worldwide.

346. In November, the brilliant red, orange and gold leaves of the bigtooth maples draw huge crowds to fall foliage tours in Lost Maples State Natural Area. The maples are said to be "lost" because they are far from any other stands of their kind, which are scattered over the western United States and northern Mexico.

347. Named for the beloved, late lieutenant governor, the Bob Bullock Texas State History Museum in Austin is a history buff's paradise. The $80 million museum houses three floors of exhibits that tell the story of Texas in painstaking detail.

348. Texas has more than 200,000 alligators.

349. Larry McMurtry's Pulitzer prize-winning novel, *Lonesome Dove*, was inspired by the life of Oliver Loving, Dean of Texas Trail Drivers.

350. And more bats…Amanda Lollar runs Bat World Living Museum in Mineral Wells where she provides a permanent sanctuary for injured, orphaned or otherwise abandoned bats.

351. Having experienced one too many house fires in their home state of Louisiana, the Bonner family settled in San Antonio in the early 1900s. Atlee B. Ayres, noted architect of the time, was commissioned to build a "fire proof house" fashioned after a 16th-century Italian villa. Built entirely of concrete and steel, the Bonner home, complete with full basement, was finished in 1909. Daughter Mary grew up in the home and became an internationally acclaimed artist and printmaker, a business run from the mansion's basement. All the rage in Europe, especially Paris, Bonner prints remain in great demand. And many of her print-making techniques are still in use today.

☆ TREMENDOUS TEXAS ☆

352. Inspired by his world travels, San Antonio artist Barney Smith has painted over 400 toilet seats! They are displayed in his garage gallery and are available for viewing anytime he is at home.

353. The Bonner mansion, listed on the National Historic Register, is located in what is now known as the Monte Vista Historical District. Lovingly restored by today's owners, Noel and Jan Stenoien, the Bonner home is now a first class bed & breakfast. For first class accommodations, and your dining pleasure, in a truly unique home, call 1-800-396-4222. They'll leave the lights on for ya!

354. After Luchenbach was made famous by Waylon Jennings' song, road signs for the city started disappearing. So many were stolen that the Texas Highway Department stopped erecting them.

☆ TREMENDOUS TEXAS ☆

SELECTED REFERENCES

World Book Encyclopedia, 2002 edition, Vol. 19.

The Texas Monthly Guidebook, 4th edition, in collaboration with Marjie Mugno Acheson...(et. al.), Gulf Publishing Company, Houston, 1998.

Texas, Nick Selby, Julie Fanselow & Ryan Van Berkmoes, Lonely Planet Publications, Victoria, Australia, 1999.

Texas Almanac 2000-2001, Millennium Edition, Mary G. Ramos, editor, Dallas: The Dallas Morning News, 1999.

USA, The Rough Guide, Samantha Cook, Tim Perry, and Greg Ward, Rough Guides Ltd., London, 2000.

The Encyclopedia Americana, Vol. 26, Grolier, Inc., Danbury, 2000.

☆ TREMENDOUS TEXAS ☆

The Western United States, Martha Ellen Zenfell, editor, Langensheidt Publishers, Inc., New York, 2000.

The Insiders' Guide to the Texas Coastal Bend, Falcon Publishing, Helena, Montana, 1998.

The Texas Hill Country Book, Berkshire House Publishers, Lee, Massachusetts, 1997.

Off the Beaten Path, June Naylor, The Globe Pequot Press, Guilford, Connecticut, 2002.

www.lsjunction.com

www.thc.state.tx.us

www.usatf.org

www.dallas-zoo.org

www.msu.edu

www.lone-star.net

☆ TREMENDOUS TEXAS ☆

http.//espn.go.com

www.tsha.utexas.edu

www.redcross.org/tx/corpuschristi

www.illustration-house.com

www.sidrmuseum.org

www.sanantoniocvb.com/visitors

www.50states.com/texas.htm

www.state.tx.us

http://gotexas.about.com

www.wacocvb.com/waco

www.hpvillage.com

www.iitexas.com

www.cs.utep.edu

☆ TREMENDOUS TEXAS ☆

www.galveston.com

www.historyhouse.com

www.palaceofwax.com

www.funtrivia.com

www.HoustonChronicle.com

www.LadyBirdJohnson.com

www.SenateKids.com

AMERICA
the *Beautiful*

Bette and George Schnitzer, Jr.